FUN AND GAMES

Building
Miniature Models

Multiplying Decimals

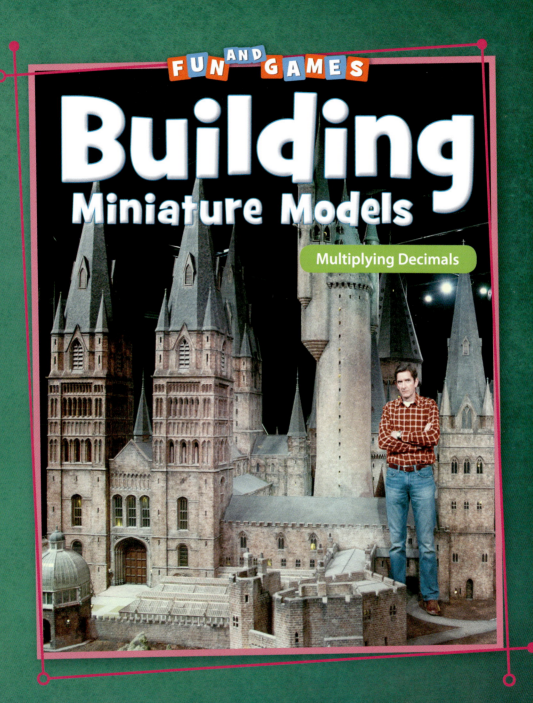

Kristy Stark, M.A.Ed.

Consultants

Lisa Ellick, M.A.
Math Specialist
Norfolk Public Schools

Pamela Estrada, M.S.Ed.
Teacher
Westminster School District

Publishing Credits

Rachelle Cracchiolo, M.S.Ed., *Publisher*
Conni Medina, M.A.Ed., *Managing Editor*
Dona Herweck Rice, *Series Developer*
Emily R. Smith, M.A.Ed., *Series Developer*
Diana Kenney, M.A.Ed., NBCT, *Content Director*
Stacy Monsman, M.A., *Editor*
Kristy Stark, M.A.Ed., *Editor*
Kevin Panter, *Graphic Designer*

Image Credits: Front cover Eamonn McCormack/WireImage; p.1 Eamonn McCormack/WireImage; p.4 Peter Lane/Alamy; p.5 Z5327 Soeren Stache Deutsch Presse Agentur/Newscom; pp6, 7 Alex Segre/Alamy; p.8 Paris Pierce/Alamy; p.9 Chronicle/Alamy; p.10 Columbia Pictures/Ronald Grant Archive/Alamy; p.11 Entertainment Pictures/Alamy; p.12 (bottom left) Granger Academic; p.13 Science Source; p.14 (bottom right) HSNPhotography/iStock; p15 (top) Andrey Khachatryan/Shutterstock; p.16 (top) Jaap2/iStock; p.16 (bottom) Bill Pugliano/Getty Images; p.20 Superelaks/Alamy; p.24 (top) Hero Images Inc/Alamy; p.25 Lifeman/Alamy; p.26 Sergei Konkov/TASS via Getty Images; p.27 (top) ChameleonsEye/Shutterstock; all other images from iStock and/or Shutterstock.

Teacher Created Materials
5301 Oceanus Drive
Huntington Beach, CA 92649-1030
http://www.tcmpub.com

ISBN 978-1-4258-5821-6

© 2018 Teacher Created Materials, Inc.
Made in China
Nordica.112017.CA21701237

Table of Contents

Miniature Models Equal Big Fun 4

The History and Purposes of Models 6

Scale Models 14

Getting Started 18

Where Will You Start? 26

Problem Solving 28

Glossary 30

Index 31

Answer Key 32

Miniature Models Equal Big Fun

Do you like to build things? Maybe you started building with blocks when you were younger. Perhaps you made tall towers and other types of buildings. Maybe you have used building bricks to make cars and airplanes.

If you enjoy building things, you may be interested in building **miniature** models. These are smaller versions of real objects. Models can be made for buildings, vehicles, airplanes, and trains. Models of landscapes can be made to show a favorite place. Some people make models of entire cities and towns, too. The possibilities are endless when it comes to the available choices of miniature models.

Building models requires many different types of skills. You might paint a model. You might need to sew fabric for parts of the model. Some models have working lights, so you might even have to wire lights to batteries.

Building miniature models, also called **scale** models, is a fun project for people who like to work with their hands and build things. But, building models is not only for people looking for a fun activity. Models are also used to create many of the things you see in the world around you.

A model-plane enthusiast works on a large-scale model aircraft in England.

Model maker Sylvia Menelao competes in a model-building contest in Germany.

The History and Purposes of Models

Throughout recorded history, scale models have been used for many things, including fun projects and many types of jobs.

Models are used to create new buildings and other structures. They are even used in the creation of movies. Models are used to show **complex** science concepts, too.

Architect Models

Architects have used models since the early fifteenth **century**. Architects build and design skyscrapers, houses, and offices. They draw building plans called **blueprints**. Then, architects build a model. Models are made before workers start laying a building's **foundation**. Models show how buildings will look when they are finished.

Construction workers use blueprints and models to understand an architect's design. Models help them see where a building's doors and windows will be placed. Models help them see the position and location of a building, too.

If models don't look right, architects know that they need to **modify** plans. Models can also help show weaknesses in the **structure** of buildings. It is **crucial** to find things that are wrong with a design before workers start building.

LET'S EXPLORE MATH

Architects use several different sizes of rectangular paper to draw blueprints. The smallest size has dimensions of about 30.5 centimeters by 22.9 centimeters. Which of the following choices is the area of the paper? Explain your reasoning.

- **A.** 6.9845 square centimeters
- **B.** 69.845 square centimeters
- **C.** 698.45 square centimeters
- **D.** 6,984.5 square centimeters

Movie Models

In 1933, the movie *King Kong* was made. It was one of the first major films to use models. In the movie, a huge gorilla wreaks havoc on New York City. A model of the giant beast was created to look like a real gorilla. The moviemakers created a model of New York City and the Empire State Building, too.

This 1933 poster advertises *King Kong*.

Throughout the history of movies, scale models have been used for special effects. Directors and producers use models to form make-believe creatures. They also use models of cities, cars, buildings, and other things that they want to destroy in a scene. Models help create the scene without destroying real objects. Models allow filmmakers to make fictional scenes look real.

The Empire State Building was the tallest building in the world at the time *King Kong* was made. The building was the focus of a famous scene in the movie. King Kong kidnaps a woman and climbs to the top of the Empire State Building. He swats at planes that circle the building as people try to rescue the woman.

This illustration shows how filmmakers used models and special effects to film *King Kong*.

A model of a marshmallow man invades New York City in this scene from *Ghostbusters*.

Since *King Kong*, lots of films have used models to show special effects. The first *Ghostbusters* movie from 1984 used models of a giant marshmallow man. The large man walks down a street in New York City. The scene has models of small cars on the street, too. These elements create the **perspective** that the man is as big as the buildings in the city.

In the 1996 film *Independence Day*, aliens invade Earth. They blow up the White House. Of course, filmmakers could not destroy the place where the president lives! So, a model was used in the scene.

Most action movies made in the past 30 years have used models of some sort. However, in recent years, more and more movies use computer-generated imagery (CGI). Computers have become more advanced. Many models are now made on computers instead of with materials. CGI software lets people build and destroy a scene without using a physical model. CGI allows more options when it comes to making movies now and in the future.

Some filmmakers may choose to use physical models to save money. Or, they may want to keep scenes simple and not have CGI images take away from the storyline. Whether it's a spaceship, a skyscraper, or an imaginary creature, mini models are a part of filmmaking that audiences have come to appreciate.

Models make it look like an alien spacecraft is targeting the White House in this scene from *Independence Day*.

This model of the solar system shows how planets orbit the sun.

J. J. Thomson

Thomson's atom model

spherical cloud of positive charge

electron

12

Scientific Models

Scientists often study things that are too small to see without powerful microscopes. They study parts of **atoms**, cells, and tiny organisms. Most people do not have the tools needed to view these things. So, scientists create models that can show people these small structures.

In 1904, J. J. Thomson made the first model of an atom. Scientists since Thomson have continued to revise his model. The updated models are more accurate based on new research. They show that a nucleus, which is the control center of a cell, is made up of protons and neutrons. The models show that electrons are outside of the nucleus. Without models of atoms, people may not be able to understand their complex structures.

Scientists have also built models of very large things. For example, the solar system is too large to see in a photo. So, models help people understand how parts of the system work together as a whole. These models show the locations and orbits of the planets. Perhaps you have even built a model of the solar system yourself for a science project.

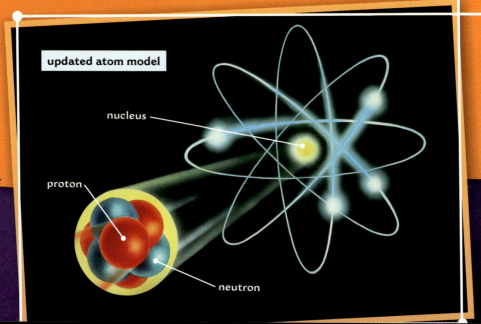

Scale Models

A scale model is a smaller version of a real thing. But, a model does not use random numbers and measurements. Instead, scale models are based on relationships. The relationships are based on the real items.

The greater a model's scale, the smaller the model will be. For instance, a model car with a 1 to 25 scale is 25 times smaller than the real car. It is much larger than a model with a 1 to 50 scale. The model with the 1 to 50 scale will be 50 times smaller than the real car!

It is important for a model builder to understand the scale of the model. It is advised that a first-time model builder start with a model that has a smaller scale. This means the model will be larger and have bigger pieces. As a builder gains experience, he or she can start to build models with a higher scale.

This model car is about two-hundredths the size of the real car.

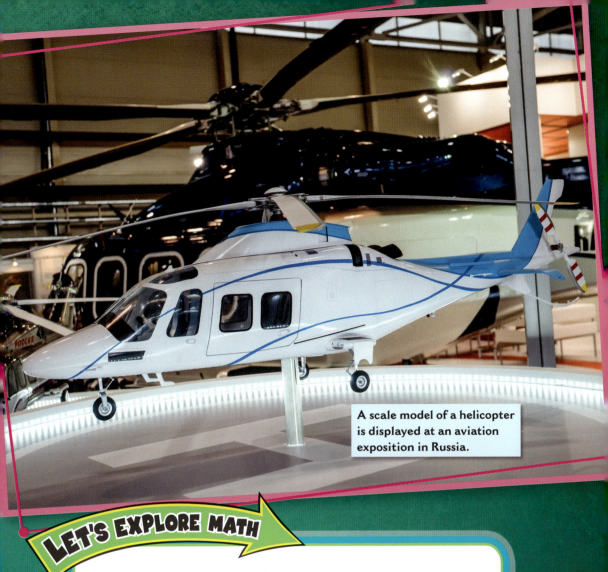

A scale model of a helicopter is displayed at an aviation exposition in Russia.

LET'S EXPLORE MATH

This radio controlled model car is 10 times smaller than the real car. Which factor can you multiply the real car's measurements by to calculate the measurements of the model? Explain your reasoning.

- **A.** 0.01
- **B.** 0.1
- **C.** 10
- **D.** 100

Car makers use a model to introduce a new car to the media in Detroit.

Model building kits use a **consistent** scale for the whole model. The model shows the real car in smaller form. So, each piece of the model car needs to have the same scale. For example, the wheels of the car cannot use a larger scale than the body of the car. If this were the case, the wheels would be disproportionate to the size of the car. The model car would not look like the real car.

Different types of models use different sizing scales. These differences date back to when the first models were produced. Each company created their models using a scale they chose. The scale usually varied from company to company.

Over the years, companies have become more consistent in using standard and widely accepted scales. But, there are still variations among different types of models. For instance, companies commonly use a 1 to 32 scale for plane models. In contrast, 1 to 43 is the most popular scale used around the world for model cars.

LET'S EXPLORE MATH

Jamie is building a model boxcar for his trainset that is 0.04 times as small as a real boxcar. Place the decimal point in the product of each equation to find the dimensions of the model boxcar.

Dimension	Real Boxcar (inches)		Model Boxcar (inches)
Length	480	× 0.04 =	192
Width	108	× 0.04 =	432
Height	96	× 0.04 =	384

A student builds a robotic vehicle model with her technology teacher.

Getting Started

Architects and scientists use models, but most miniature models are built by ordinary people. It is such a popular hobby that you can find model kits, tools, and materials in most craft and hobby stores.

It can be a **daunting** task to start a new hobby or project. But, with some preparation and thought, you can be organized and ready to start building.

Find a Workspace

The first step to getting started is to find a good workspace for building. The workspace should be a place where you can organize your tools and materials. The space should have enough room to work without having to move things around to create more space.

Your workspace should be in an area where you will not bother other people. Building models takes time and involves a lot of small parts. You need to make sure that your materials will not get in the way of other family members. You also don't want younger brothers or sisters to get ahold of small pieces.

You also want a workspace that you do not have to take apart every day. You need to find a place where you can work for several days or weeks. You should be able to tidy up every day without having to move everything.

A workbench in a garage can be a good space to build.

Gather Tools and Materials

Once you have a space to work, you can gather the tools and materials you will need to build. The necessary tools depend on whether you are building a model from a kit or from scratch. If you purchase a kit, some materials will be in the box. You may need to purchase glue and paint if they are not included.

If you build a model from scratch, you may need a small screwdriver and screws or a hammer and nails. You will likely need glue and paint, too. Find a small bin or shoebox to help you store your tools and supplies. That way, you will always be able to find what you need when you need it.

LET'S EXPLORE MATH

The rectangular surface of Lena's workbench is 0.7 meters long and 1.2 meters wide. Complete the strategy shown to find its area.

$0.7 \times 1.2 = ($ _____ $\times 1) + (0.7 \times$ _____ $)$

$= $ _____ $+$ _____

$= $ _____ square meters

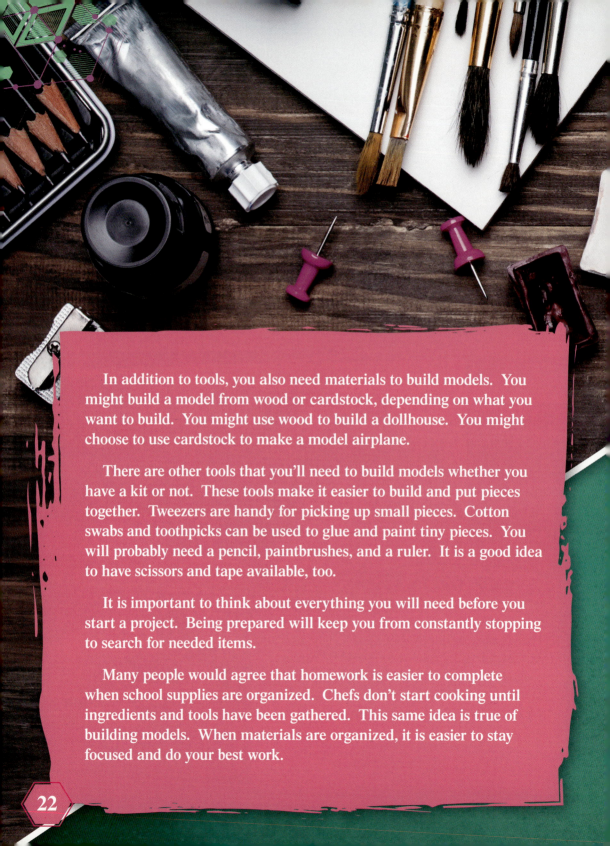

In addition to tools, you also need materials to build models. You might build a model from wood or cardstock, depending on what you want to build. You might use wood to build a dollhouse. You might choose to use cardstock to make a model airplane.

There are other tools that you'll need to build models whether you have a kit or not. These tools make it easier to build and put pieces together. Tweezers are handy for picking up small pieces. Cotton swabs and toothpicks can be used to glue and paint tiny pieces. You will probably need a pencil, paintbrushes, and a ruler. It is a good idea to have scissors and tape available, too.

It is important to think about everything you will need before you start a project. Being prepared will keep you from constantly stopping to search for needed items.

Many people would agree that homework is easier to complete when school supplies are organized. Chefs don't start cooking until ingredients and tools have been gathered. This same idea is true of building models. When materials are organized, it is easier to stay focused and do your best work.

A father and daughter work together to build a model.

LET'S EXPLORE MATH

Bridget's dad helps her build furniture for her dollhouse. The dollhouse furniture is 0.08 times as small as real furniture.

1. The real kitchen table is 0.7 meters tall. How tall is the dollhouse kitchen table (in meters)?

2. The real kitchen chair's seat height is 0.4 meters. What is the seat height for the dollhouse kitchen chair (in meters)?

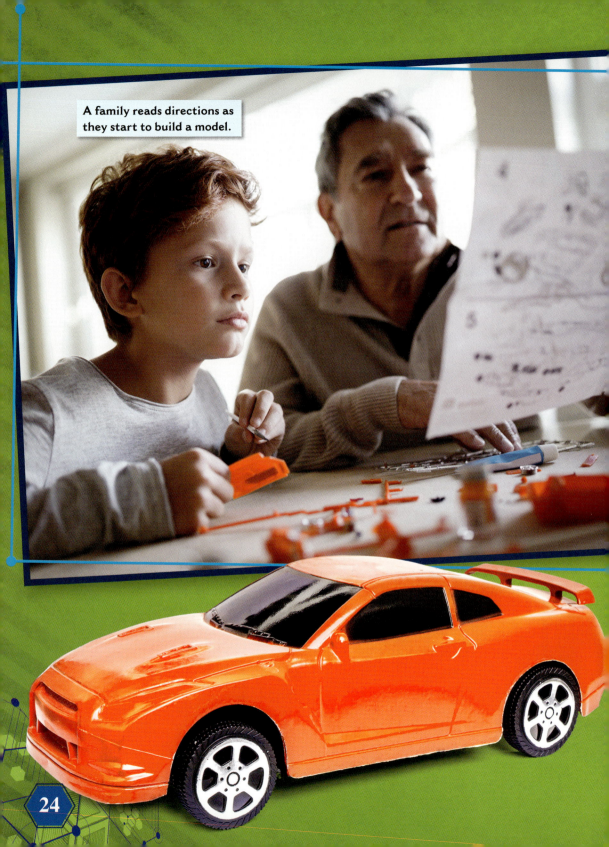

A family reads directions as they start to build a model.

Read and Follow Instructions

It is important to follow directions when building models. Directions are like blueprints that architects create and use. Blueprints show exactly how structures should look when finished. Directions must be followed for buildings or models to turn out the correct way.

If you use a kit, directions will be included in the box. The plans will have pictures that show how the completed model will look. There will be pictures that show each step of the building process. There will be step-by-step written directions, too.

Carefully read the instructions before you start working. The plans will give you a list of materials and tools that you will need.

If you make a model from scratch, you can find building plans for many types of models on the Internet. Or, you can design and draw your own plans for the model you intend to make. For your first project, start with a model that has simple plans.

Whether you use printed directions or make your own, start with a clear plan before you begin building your model.

This model kit has many pieces that have to be organized and assembled.

Where Will You Start?

Some people like the challenge of building something by hand. They enjoy working hard to finish a project. Many people display models in their homes as a reminder of their hard work. They are proud of what they've built.

Some people also want to interact with other model builders. There are clubs and organizations that people can join. This is a way to meet people who have the same hobby. They can admire other people's hard work. They may share tips they have learned over the years. They may share suggestions for how new builders can get started.

A museum worker builds a scale model that is about one-hundredth the size of real landmarks in Russia.

Members of a model boat club meet to sail their creations.

Many of these organizations have conventions. Conventions are events where people with common interests can meet one another and learn. Model conventions give people a place to buy new model kits and meet other model builders. People can see **elaborate** model displays, too.

If you want to start making models, you might want to find a club in your local area. A simple Internet search will likely **yield** many results showing clubs in your area. There are clubs for people who build model trains. There are other clubs for people who build military models. Whatever your preference, you could quickly become a master model maker.

LET'S EXPLORE MATH

Paolo is a member of a model boat club. He is buying sail cloth which is sold by the square meter.

1. Paolo needs a rectangular piece of sail cloth with a length of 0.8 meters and width of 0.5 meters. How many square meters of cloth will he buy?

2. Sail cloth is $30 per square meter.

    a. Will Paolo's cloth cost more or less than $30? How do you know?

    b. How much will Paolo's cloth cost?

27

Problem Solving

Arthur is building a scale model of a rock formation and medieval tower for his social studies class. He is deciding whether to build a model that is 0.1 times as small or 0.01 times as small as the real formation and tower. Help him decide by calculating the measurements for each feature and answering the questions.

1. What patterns do you see in the table? Why do you think this happens?

2. Arthur's rectangular display board has a length of 0.8 meters and width of 0.75 meters. What is the area of the display board?

3. Which scale model do you recommend Arthur build? Why?

Feature	Actual Measurements (meters)	Scale Model Measurements (meters)	
		0.1 Times as Small	0.01 Times as Small
Rock formation height	41.5		
Tower length	2.7		
Tower width	3.6		
Tower height	19.8		

Glossary

architects—people who design buildings

atoms—the smallest parts of a substance

blueprints—detailed plans for a building

century—a time period of 100 years

complex—not easy to understand or explain

consistent—continues to happen in the same way

crucial—very important

daunting—very difficult to deal with

elaborate—made with great care and detail

foundation—concrete structure that a building is built on

miniature—small

modify—change

perspective—depth or distance of objects in relation to other objects

scale—the size of something in comparison to something else

structure—the way something is built, organized, or arranged

yield—to produce

Index

architect, 6–7, 18, 25

atom, 12–13

blueprints, 6–7, 25

building plans, 6, 25

computer-generated imagery (CGI), 10

Empire State Building, 8–9

foundation, 6

Ghostbusters, 10

Independence Day, 10–11

King Kong, 8–10

kits, 17–18, 21–22, 25, 27

materials, 10, 18–19, 21–22, 25, 28

microscope, 13

New York City, 8, 10

scale, 4, 6, 9, 14–17, 28

solar system, 12–13

Thomson, J. J., 12–13

tools, 13, 18–19, 21–23, 25, 28

workspace, 19–20

Answer Key

Let's Explore Math

page 7:

C; Explanations will vary but may include using estimation to show that 30 × 20 is 600, so the most reasonable answer must be around 600 square centimeters.

page 15:

B; Explanations will vary but may include that 0.1 is equal to one-tenth, so multiplying real measurements by this factor will result in scaled measurements that are 10 times as small.

page 17:

19.2; 4.32; 3.84

page 21:

0.84 sq. m; 0.7; 0.2; 0.7; 0.14; 0.84

page 23:

1. 0.056 m
2. 0.032 m

page 27:

1. 0.4 sq. m
2. a. Less than $30; He is buying less than 1 sq. m of sail cloth, so it must cost less than $30.
   b. $12

Problem Solving

Rock formation height: 4.15 m; 0.415 m

Tower length: 0.27 m; 0.027 m

Tower width: 0.36 m; 0.036 m

Tower height: 1.98 m; 0.198 m

1. The decimal point moves to the left each time because the products are ten times smaller.
2. 0.6 sq. m
3. Answers will vary. Example: The scale model that is 0.01 times as small is the best choice because it has measurements that are more reasonable to fit on a display board and take to school.